More French for Little Girls

A French language workbook for little girls

Written and Illustrated by: Yvonne Crawford

www.languageforlittlelearners.com

About this workbook

This book is a continuation of French for Little Girls. In this second level your daughter will continue her exploration of the French language while engaging in activities that will help to motivate her. She will pretend to be a baby animal, dress up like a fairy, play with paper dolls and more.

This workbook is created especially for parents who do not have any prior knowledge of French. You and your daughter can embark on a journey of learning a foreign language together. Everything you need is inside this workbook, including a pronunciation guide, dictionary and teaching hints.

Every lesson will consist of a list of vocabulary words with pictures, three activities your daughter can do in the workbook with your guidance and two activities you can do together without the workbook for further practice. Each new word that is introduced will have its pronunciation next to it.

In the appendices there is a learning slide that your daughter can color after she completes each lesson. This will help your child to visualize and take pride in her progress.

Try not to put stress on your daughter to have perfect pronunciation or to remember every single word. If she forgets a word, simply repeat it and then use it in a sentence a few times; eventually she will catch on. It is important for her (and you) to have a positive first experience with learning a foreign language. It will encourage her to continue and succeed in the future with more language studies.

Table of Contents

Leçon 1
Art Girls

Vocabulary:

l'artiste *lahr-teest*
artist

le sculpteur *luh-scoolp-tuhr*
sculptor

le pinceau
luh-pahn-soh
paint brush

la peintre *lah-payntr*
painter

la peinture *lah-payn-tuhr*
paint

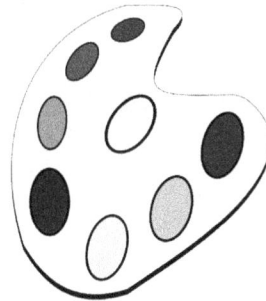

le crayon *luh-kray-yohn*
pencil

Fun Phrases:

oui	*wee*	yes
non	*nòh*	no
peut-être	*puht-ehtr*	maybe

Teaching Tips:

- Throughout the day, ask your children questions in either French or English and then prompt them to answer you in French with the words they have learned above for yes, no and maybe.

- If your child asks you what a word is in French that is not listed in this book, look it up in a French/English dictionary or on a website and then create a little dictionary for them out of a small spiral notebook. You can even have them draw the picture in the notebook in order to help them to remember the word.

Activité Une

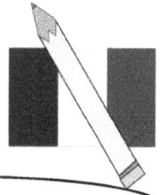

Bonjour! My name is Lilou. It's nice to meet you. Can you match the picture to the correct French word?

le sculpteur

la peintre

l'artiste

Activité Deux

Now you can greet each of my friends in French! For each picture above, say *'Bonjour'*, then say their name.

Activité Trois

Tell me which of these things you like. If you like them then write *oui,* and if you don't like them, write *non*.

J'aime... I like...

_____

_ _ _ _ _ _ _ _ _ _ _ _ _ _

_____

_ _ _ _ _ _ _ _ _ _ _ _ _ _

_____

_ _ _ _ _ _ _ _ _ _ _ _ _ _

_____

_ _ _ _ _ _ _ _ _ _ _ _ _ _

_____

_____

Activité Quatre

Yes, No, or Maybe?

Throughout the day, use your French whenever you can! When your mom or dad asks you a question, say the answer in French. Use: *oui*, *non*, or *peut-être*. Every time you say one of these words today, you can come back to this workbook and record it on this page. Color a star each time you use one of your new French words.

oui   *non*   *peut-être*

☆ ☆ ☆ ☆ ☆ ☆ ☆ ☆ ☆

Activité Cinq

Pencil Toss

What you will need:
construction paper
scissors
pencil
cardboard
cap or cup

What to do:
1. Draw and cut out 10 pencils. You can trace the one from the workbook if you would like.
2. Glue the cut-out pencils to the cardboard and get your mother or father to help you cut them out.
3. Toss the pretend pencils into the cap or cup and count them in French as you do. *Un crayon, deux crayons,* etc.

Leçon 2
Silly Faces

Vocabulary:

les cheveux
lay-shuh-vuh
hair

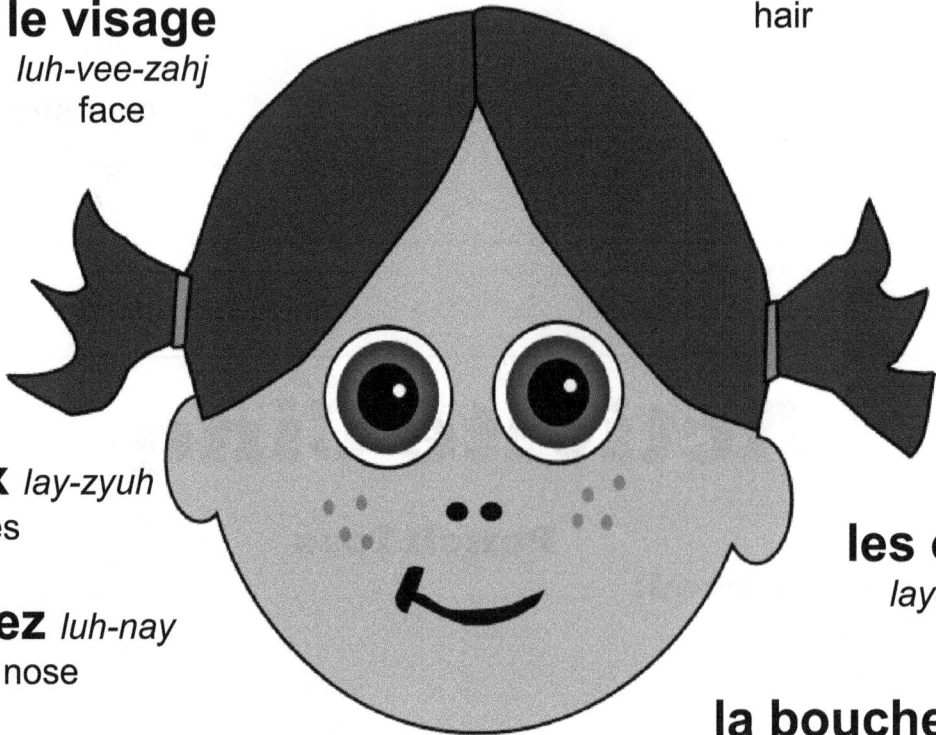

le visage
luh-vee-zahj
face

les yeux *lay-zyuh*
eyes

le nez *luh-nay*
nose

les oreilles
lay-zoh-ray
ears

la bouche
lah-boosh
mouth

je suis en colère
zhuh-sweez-ahn-koh-lehr
I'm angry

je suis fou
zhuh-swee-foo
I'm crazy

12

je suis triste
zhuh-swee-treest
I'm sad

je suis contente
zhuh-swee-kohn-tahnt
I'm happy

Fun Phrase:

très	*trey*	very

Teaching Tips:

- Go through the lessons as fast or as slow as your child wants to go. Look to her for signs of fatigue. There is always tomorrow where you can take up where you left off today.

- Feel free to go back to the first level of French for Little Girls in case your daughter has forgotten things like colors or numbers in French. It's a good idea to go back and review previous topics.

Activité Une

Come and meet some of my friends. Each of them is missing one part of their faces. Say the name of the facial part that is missing in French and then draw the missing parts onto their faces.

Activité Deux

Oh no! One of my friends had to go away on vacation and she was supposed to spend the day with me. Can you draw me a friend? As you draw the different body and facial parts, say their names in French. Make sure to use colors and say the colors' names in French, too.

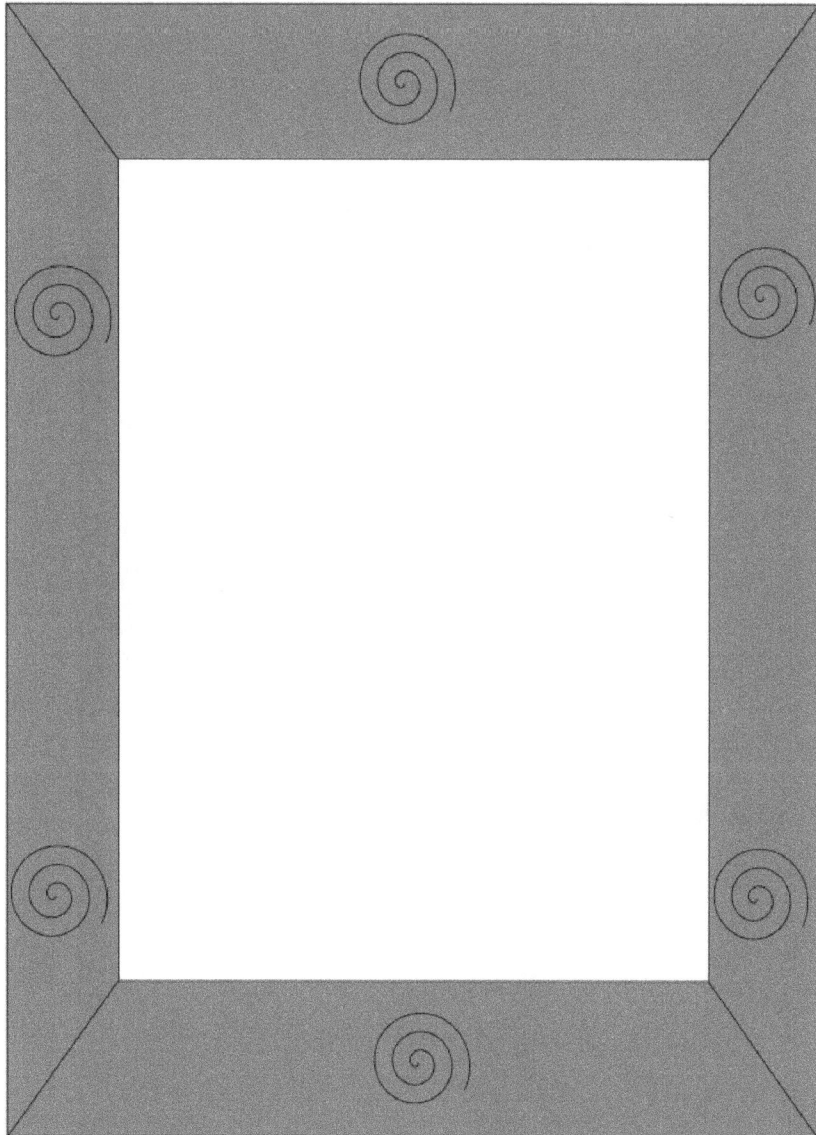

Activité Trois

Match the French word to the picture of the correct facial part.

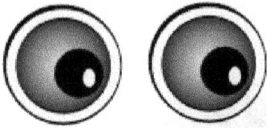
les oreilles

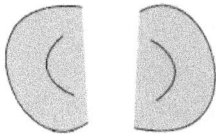
les cheveux

le nez

les yeux

la bouche

Activité Quatre

Drawing Faces

What you will need:

paper
pencil

What to do:

1. Draw one facial part on a piece of paper.
2. Have your siblings or parents guess what it is. Tell them the name in French.
3. Switch roles; now you guess what they are drawing. Say the word in French.
4. Keep on playing, switching roles after each turn.

Activité Cinq

Different Faces

What you will need:

your mom, dad or sibling

What to do:

1. Your mom or dad will make a face.
2. In French describe how the face is. Is it a sad face? A mad face? A crazy face? If so, say the names in French.
3. Switch roles with your parent. Now it is your turn to make silly faces and your parents can describe them in French.

Leçon 3

Dress Up

Vocabulary:

les bijoux *lay-bee-zhoo*
jewelry

le collier *luh-koh-lee-ay*
necklace

le bracelet
luh-bras-leht
bracelet

l'anneau *lah-noh*
ring

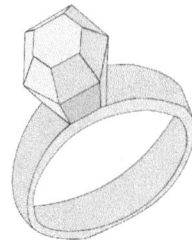

**la boucle
d'oreille**
lah-boo-kluh-doh-ray
earring

11 **onze** *ohnz*
eleven

12 **douze** *dooz*
twelve

13 **treize** *trehz*
thirteen

14 **quatorze** *ka-tohrz*
fourteen

15 **quinze** *kanz*
fifteen

Teaching Tips:

- It's easy for children to learn numbers in order. It is much more difficult for them to be able to say them out-of-order. Make sure you help your daughter practice her numbers both ways.

Activité Une

Count the different objects in French, then write the number in the box.

Activité Deux

Color the picture according the codes at the bottom of the page.

12

11

15 15

11

14

13

color key	
onze - bleu	quatorze - noir
douze - vert	quinze - rouge
treize - orange	

Activité Trois

Match the number to the word in French. Then, write French number in the space provided.

15

| douze | ____ ____ ____ ____ |

13

| quatorze | ____ ____ ____ ____ |

11

| treize | ____ ____ ____ ____ |

12

| quinze | ____ ____ ____ ____ |

14

| onze | ____ ____ ____ ____ |

Activité Quatre

Counting in Twos and Fives

Practice your French numbers by counting by twos, and by fives. By doing this, you'll be able to remember all of the numbers more quickly. You can practice by counting your toys and grouping them first into sets of twos, and then by fives. Have fun!

2, 4, 6, 8, 10, 12, 14!

Activité Cinq

Playing Dress up

What you will need:
any jewelry that you have
any jewelry that your mother will let you borrow
fancy clothes

What to do:
1. Put on some jewelry and fancy clothes.
2. Go to your mom or dad and describe all of the *bijoux* that you have on.
3. Change your *bijoux* and outfit.
4. Go back to your mom or dad and describe your *bijoux* again.
5. Continue as long as you are having fun. Make sure to use your French!

Leçon 4
Polite Fairies

Vocabulary:

la fée *lah-fay*
fairy

l'aile *lehl*
wing

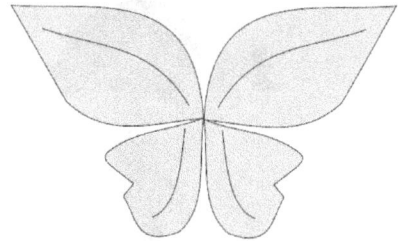

la poussière magique
lah-poo-syehr-mah-jeek
magic dust

le baguette
luh-bah-geht
wand

Fun Phrases:

enchanté	ahn-shahn-tay	nice to meet you
excusez-moi	ehks-kyoo-zay-mwah	excuse me
bon appétit	bohn-ap-pay-tee	have a good meal
à tes souhaits	a-tay-soo-ayt	bless you (said after a sneeze)

Activité Une

 Look at the pictures below. Draw a line from each picture to the correct phrase in French.

à tes souhaits

enchanté

bon appétit

Activité Deux

Please help the fairy find her way to her *baguette*. As you pass each person on the maze, make sure you say *excusez-moi,* to be polite.

Activité Trois

Look at each picture below. Draw a line under your favorite item and say its name in French. Next, draw a circle around your least favorite item and say its name in French. Finally, circle your mother's or father's favorite item in *bleu* and say its name in French.

Activité Quatre

I'm a Fairy!

Dress up as a fairy and practice all of your favorite polite French phrases. Say things like *"bon appétit!"* before your afternoon snack. Be creative; if you don't have a fairy costume, use some paper and make yourself some wings. Also, you can create a wand out of an empty paper towel roll and paper. Have fun!

Activité Cinq

Fairy and Dress Up Bingo

What you will need:
the bingo cards and calling cards from the appendix of this book
a marker for the bingo cards - pennies or small stones
a hat or cap

What to do:
1. Your mother or father can cut the calling cards from the back of the book and put them inside a hat.
2. One by one they will draw one piece of paper from the hat and say the word on the paper in French.
3. Each time you hear a word, you look at your bingo card and try to find the picture. Place a marker on the spot if you have a match.
4. When you get 5 in a row, you win and you can shout out "BINGO!"
5. Try playing with a friend or a sibling and see who can win first!

BINGO!

BINGO

Leçon 5
Baby Animals

Vocabulary:

le chaton
luh-sha-tohn
kitten

le chiot
luh-shee-oh
puppy

le veau
luh-voh
calf

le poussin
luh-poo-sehn
chick

le poulain
luh-poo-lahn
foal

seize *sehz*
sixteen
16

dix-sept *dees-seht*
seventeen
17

dix-huit
deez-*weet*
eighteen
18

dix-neuf
deez-*neuhf*
nineteen
19

vingt *vahnt*
twenty
20

Activité Une

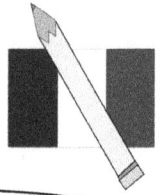

Bonjour! Look at the picture below. How many of my *chiot* friends can you find? Try to find 20. As you find each one, circle it in *rouge* and count each one in French.

Activité Deux

Use your crayon and connect all of the dots to finish his picture. As you connect the dots say each number in French!

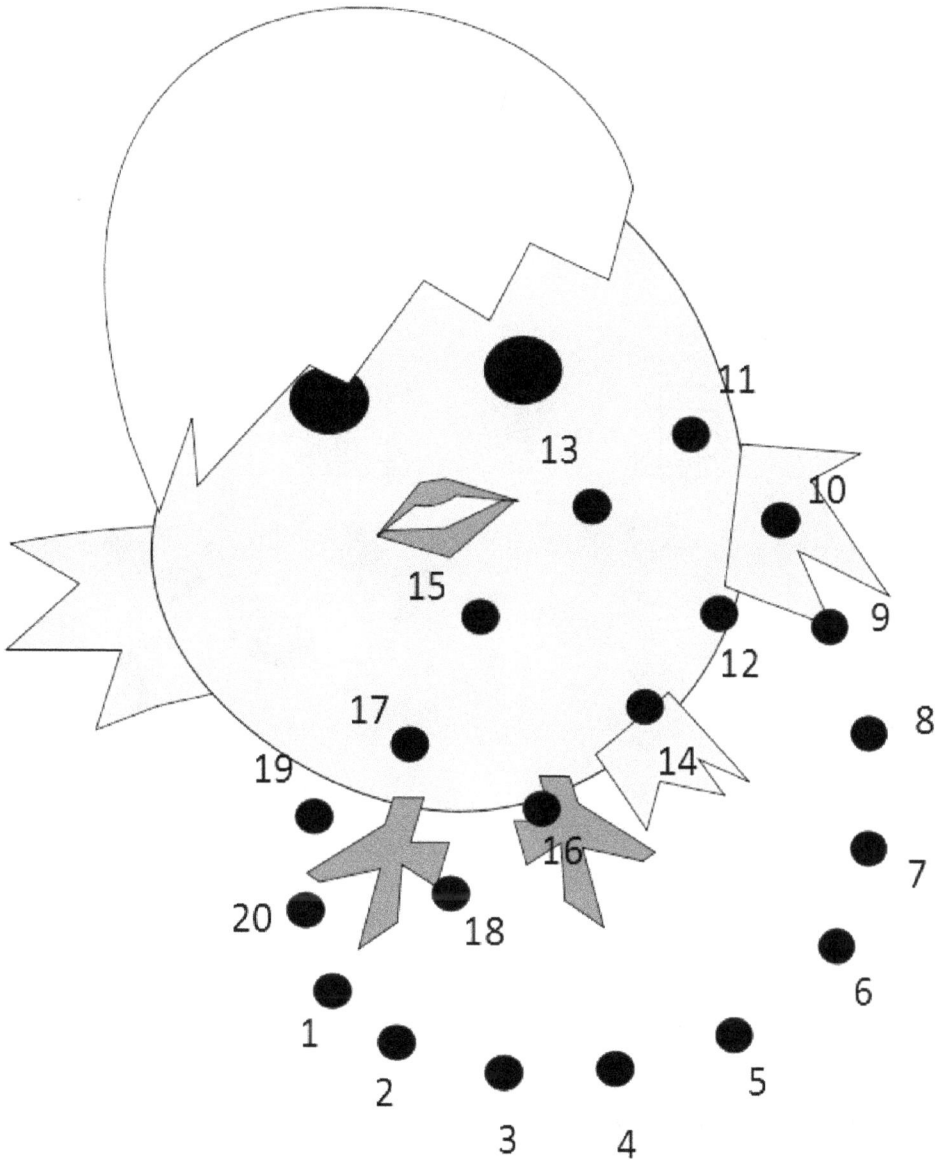

11

13

10

15

9

12

17

8

19

14

16

20

18

7

1

6

2

5

3   4

Activité Trois

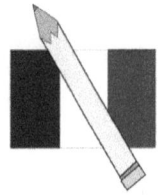

Count the pictures below in French, and then circle the correct number.

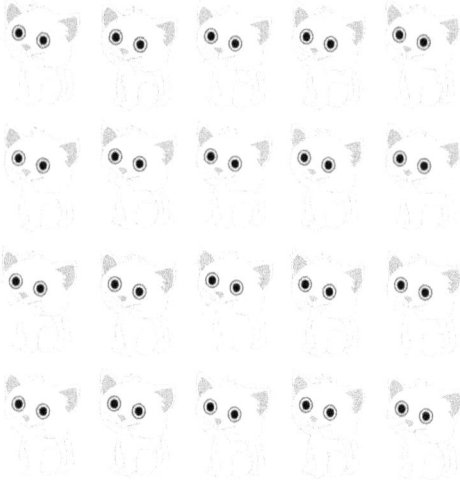

20	19	18

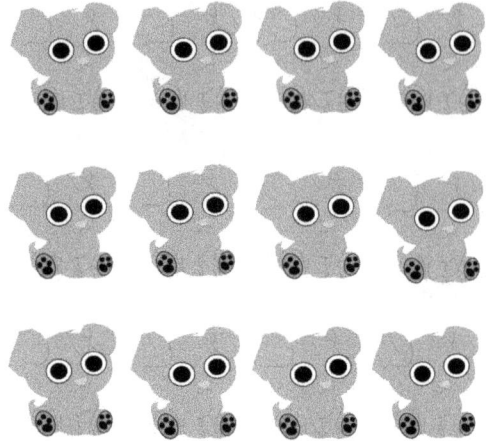

15	14	12

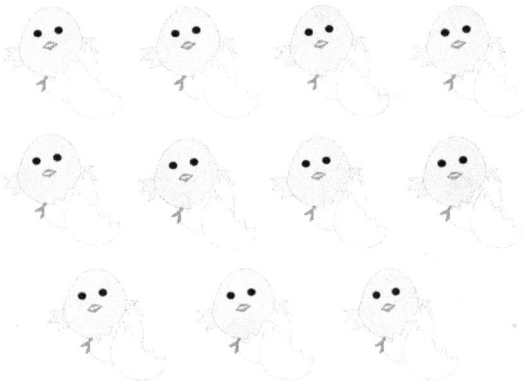

12	11	13

12	13	11

Challenge:

Start a collection of objects! Brainstorm with your parent about different things that could be in your collection (dolls, stickers, sea shells, pencils, stamps, postcards). After gathering the objects for your collection, count the number of items in your collection in French. Try to find at least 20 for your collection.

Activité Quatre

Pet Masks

What you will need:

paper plates
scissors
glue
crayons
yarn

What to do:

1. Ask your mom or dad to help you draw a baby animal face on a paper plate.
2. Cut out and color the mask.
3. Tie yarn on it so that you can wear it.
4. Pretend to be that animal and show all of your friends. Teach them the pet's name in French.

Activité Cinq

A Dice Game

What you will need:

dice (3 or 4)
paper
pencil

What to do:

1. Roll the dice and count in French how many dots you have.
2. Let the next person roll the dice and then they will count how many dots they have in French.
3. Write down on the piece of paper who won that round and keep playing until one person wins 10 games.

Challenge:

Learn to count higher in French and play the game with four dice.
21- vingt-et-un   22 - vingt-deux   23 - vingt-trois   24 - vingt-quatre

Leçon 6

Fun Sports

Vocabulary:

le football
luh-foot-ball
soccer

le vélo *luh-vay-loh*
cycling

la natation
lah-nah-tah-seeohn
swimming

le patinage sur glace
luh-pa-tee-nahj-suhr-glass
ice skating

la gymnastique
lah-zhim-nahs-teek
gymnastics

le tennis
luh-teh-nees
tennis

Fun Phrases:

je joue	*zhuh-zhoo*	I play
tu joues	*too-zhoo*	you play

Teaching Tips:

- Usually, when you want to tell someone you play a sport, you need to put '*à*' in front of the sport's name.
- Please note that *à* + *le* = *au*
- For some sports you need to use the verb '*faire*' instead of *jouer*. Then, you put '*de*' before the sport's name.
- Please note that *de* + *le* = *du*
- Here are some sentences to help you learn when to use which word:

Je joue au basket. - I play basketball.
Je joue au football. - I play soccer.

***

Je fais du vélo. - I bike.
Je fais de la natation or Je nage. - I swim.

Activité Une

Draw a line from the sport, to the sport name in French.

le vélo

la gymnas-tique

le patinage sur glace

la natation

le tennis

Activité Deux

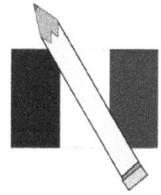

Circle the six differences between the two pictures. As you find each difference, count the number in French.

Activité Trois

Answer the questions below about the sports that you play. Circle *oui* for yes and *non* for no.

1. Do you like to play "*le football*"?	Oui	Non
2. Have you ever played "*le tennis*"?	Oui	Non
3. Do you like to "*faire du vélo*"?	Oui	Non
4. Do you like to watch "*le patinage sur glace*"?	Oui	Non

Now, draw a picture of your favorite sport. Write the name of the sport on the line below the picture frame.

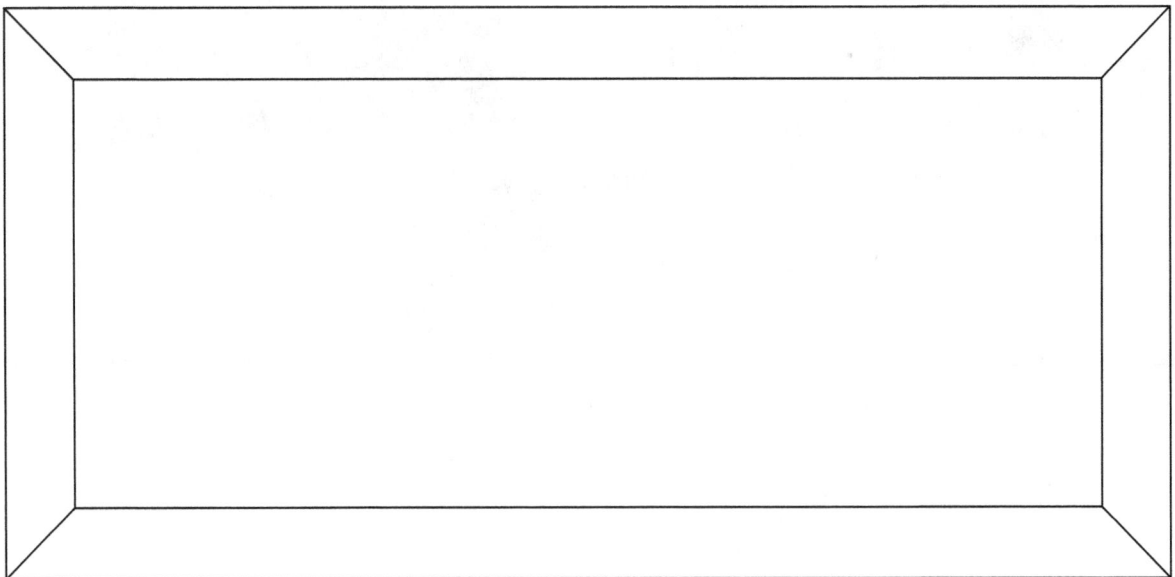

_____

Activité Quatre

Sports Charades

What you will need:

paper
pencils
cap or hat

What to do:

1. Write down each sport name on a small piece of paper.
2. Fold each piece of paper and place it in the hat.
3. Draw a piece of paper out of the hat and act it out.
4. Everyone will guess what you are acting out, saying the name in French.
5. Change roles and keep on playing.

Challenge:

Make complete sentences to guess what sport the person is acting out. You can say things like: *Tu fais de la natation.*

Activité Cinq

Tennis Numbers

What you will need:

10 tennis balls or another type of small ball
paper
tape
scissors
2 hats or caps

13

What to do:

1. Cut out 10 small pieces of paper and write one number on each piece of paper (11 to 20).
2. Tape one piece of paper to each ball.
3. Put all of the balls in one hat and put the other hat across the room.
4. Pull out one ball at a time and say the number in French, then throw it into the other hat. If you make it, you score a point. Good Luck!

Leçon 7

Dance Time

Vocabulary:

le ballet *leh-bah-lay*
ballet

le justaucorps
luh-just-oh-kohr
leotard

la danse jazz
lah-dahns-jazz
jazz dance

les chaussures de ballet
lay-show-soohrs-duh-bah-lay
ballet shoes

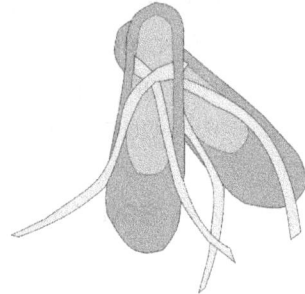

la danse du robinet
lah-dahns-doo-roh-bee-nay
tap dance

Fun Phrases:

je danse	*zhuh-dahns*	I dance
tu danses	*too-dahns*	you dance
danser	*dahn-say*	to dance
je veux	*zhuh-vuh*	I want
tu veux	*too-vuh*	you want
faire	*fair*	to make/to do
la danse	*lah-dahns*	dance

Challenge:

- You can help your child form questions using the new verbs listed above:

    Qu'est-ce que tu veux faire? - What do you want to do?

- Remember to teach these lessons as slowly or as quickly as your child is comfortable with. If your child is not ready for this challenge, you can always come back to it at a later time.

Activité Une

Look at the picture of the girl at her dance recital. Color all of the parts of the picture according to the color key below.

12

15

16   11   18

17

13

20

douze	rouge	onze	noir
dix-sept	blanc	dix-huit	bleu
treize	vert	quinze	orange
seize	noir	vingt	rouge

Activité Deux

Answer the questions by drawing a picture in the box below each question or circling the answer. (que or qu'=what; quelle=which)

1. *Qu'est-ce que tu veux faire?*

2. Draw your perfect *justaucorps*. Design it anyway you want!

3. *Est-ce que tu veux danser?*   *Oui*   *Non*

4. *Quelle danse?* Draw yourself performing the dance in the box.

Activité Trois

Can you help me explain what I want to do and what I don't want to do? Circle the correct French sentence for each picture.

Je veux danser.

Je ne veux pas danser.

Je veux faire de la gymnastique.

Je ne veux pas faire de la gymnastique.

Je veux danser.

Je ne veux pas danser.

Activité Quatre

Crazy Dancing

What you will need:

CD player or radio
dance outfit or some fun clothes

What to do:

1. Dress up in your favorite dance outfit.
2. Say *"Je veux danser!"* so that your parent can start the music playing.
3. After a little while, they will turn off the music.
4. When you want them to start the music again, tell them that you want to dance in French again.
5. Keep on dancing and having fun!

Challenge:

Reverse the game and say "Je ne veux pas danser!" when you want your parents to turn off the music.

Activité Cinq

My Book of Wants

What you will need:

old magazines
scissors
glue stick
paper
yarn

What to do:

1. With your mom or dad's help, create a little booklet out of paper by folding paper in half and fastening it with yarn.
2. On the cover of the booklet write: *Je veux*... (I want...)
3. Look through magazines and cut out pictures of things you would like one day.
4. You can also draw pictures of things you want.

Leçon 8
A Day at the Beach

Vocabulary:

la plage *lah-plahj*
beach

la ballon de plage
lah-ba-lohn-duh-plahj
beach ball

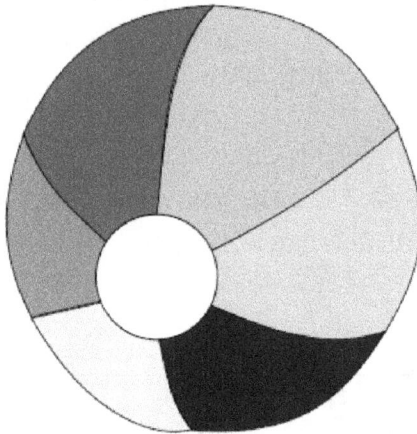

la mer
lah-mehr
sea

la coquille
lah-koh-keel
shell

les lunettes de soleil
lay-loo-neht-duh-soh-lay
sunglasses

le sable *luh-sah-bl*
sand

le château de sable
luh-shah-toh-duh-sah-bl
sandcastle

Fun Phrases:

je nage	*zhuh-nahj*	I swim
tu nages	*too-nahj*	you swim

Teaching Tips:

- As your child learns new French vocabulary, try to have her remember to use the article with the noun.

  le - masculine or *la* - feminine

Activité Une

Come join me at the beach! Look at the picture below. Point to items in the picture and say their names in French. Each time you say a name in French, color the object.

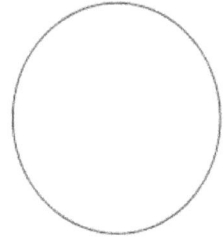

Activité Deux

Draw a line from the phrase in English to the phrase in French. Then, draw a picture describing the phrase.

je nage

I swim

you swim

tu nages

I swim

you swim

Activité Trois

Draw a line from the picture to the correct word in French. Make sure to say the French word out loud as you are drawing the line.

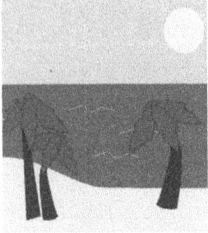

la boule de plage

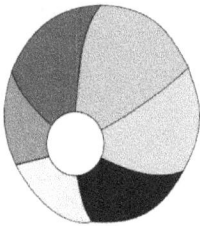

la coquille

la plage

le sable

la mer

Activité Quatre

Counting *Coquilles*

What you will need:

many *coquilles* or a trip to the beach
bucket

What to do:

Option 1:

Take a trip to a beach. Pick up as many shells as you can find and put them in your bucket. Every time you pick one up, count it in French.

Option 2:

Take all of the shells that you have collected on a previous trip to the beach and give them to your parents. Let them hide the shells around your house or backyard. You can then search for the *coquilles*. Every time you find a shell count it in French.

Activité Cinq

A Sandy Picture

What you will need:

a little bit of sand
paper
markers, crayons or paint
glue stick

What to do:

1. Make your own beach picture.
2. Draw all of the items that are listed in this lesson (get your parent to help you if you need help). As you draw each object, say its name in French.
3. Color all of the items except for the sand.
4. Rub the glue stick on the part of the picture that is sand.
5. Sprinkle sand on the glue and let dry.
6. Dust off remaining sand and hang up your picture. Every time you walk by your picture, point to the items and say their names in French.

Leçon 9
Cooking in the Kitchen

Vocabulary:

le boulanger
luh-boo-lahn-zhay
baker

le cuisinier
luh-kwee-zee-nyehr
cook

le petit déjeuner
luh-peh-tee-day-zhuh-nay
breakfast

le déjeuner
luh-day-zhuh-nay
lunch

le dîner
luh-dee-nay
dinner

le dessert
luh-deh-sehr
dessert

Fun Phrases:

je cuisine	*zhuh-kwee-zeen*	I cook
tu cuisines	*too-kwee-zeen*	you cook
la cuisine	*lah-kwee-zeen*	kitchen

Challenge:

If you think your daughter is ready for some grammar, you can introduce the past tense in French. This is a very brief introduction of one form of past tense in French.

The French language has a few different past tenses. The one that is introduced in this lesson is called *passé composé*. Generally, it is used to describe an action that has been fully completed. Passé composé is formed by using one of 2 auxiliary verbs: avoir (to have) or être (to be). The verb in this lesson use the first auxiliary verb, avoir. The auxiliary verb is conjugated in the present tense. Then, you put the action verb into the past participle. The past participle for cook (cuisiner) is cuisiné. Putting the two words together gives you the passé composé.

J'ai cuisiné - I cooked.
Tu as cuisiné - You cooked.

Activité Une

Circle the correct word for each picture.

| le dîner | le petit déjeuner |

| le déjeuner | le dîner |

| le petit déjeuner | le déjeuner |

Activité Deux

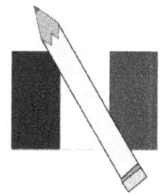

Who is cooking breakfast? Trace the lines to figure out who is cooking breakfast. Then, on the line at the bottom of the page, write the name of the person who is cooking breakfast and then rewrite the whole sentence.

Lilou

Laure

Carole

_____ cuisine.

_____

Activité Trois

Ask your mom or dad to help you read these questions. Then, circle your answer for each question.

Have you ever made your own *déjeuner*?

oui   *non*

Which is your favorite meal of the day?

le dîner   *le déjeuner*   *le petit déjeuner*

Which of these do you help your parents to make?

le petit déjeuner   *le dessert*

Which would you rather be?

le boulanger   *le cuisinier*

Activité Quatre

Which Meal?

What you will need:
play food or pictures of food
paper bag

What to do:
1. Put your play food into the paper bag and shake it up.
2. Take one piece out of the bag and say for which meal you would eat it. For example: If you take an egg out of the bag, you can say, "*petit déjeuner*".

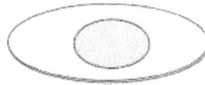

Note: Of course, some types of food can be eaten at more than one meal. That's okay, just pick one.

Activité Cinq

Cooking with Mom

What you will need:
a simple recipe that you can cook with your mother or father
any ingredients and/or supplies you will need to make your recipe

What to do:
1. Start helping your mom cook the recipe. When you are helping say, "*Je cuisine.*"
2. When your mother takes over for some steps, say, "*Tu cuisines.*"
3. Keep saying both sentences as you finish cooking the recipe.

Leçon 10
Paper Dolls

Vocabulary:

le chemise
luh-sheh-meez
shirt

le pantalon
luh-pahn-tah-lohn
pants

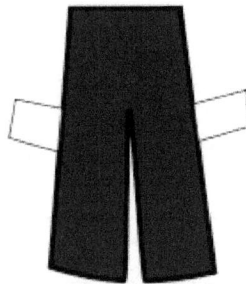

la robe
lah-rohb
dress

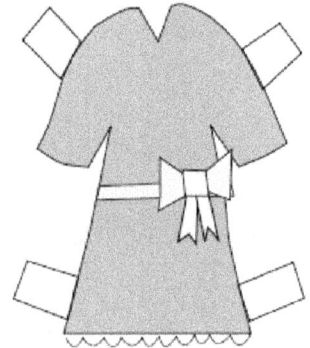

la jupe
lah-zhoop
skirt

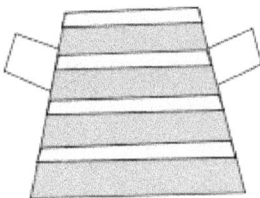

le manteau
luh-mahn-toh
coat

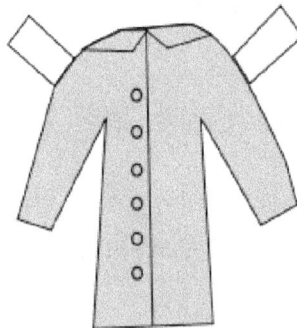

le chapeau
luh-shah-poh
hat

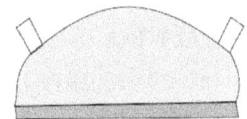

Activité Une

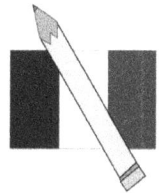

Oops, my friend Laure got caught out in the rain and now her clothes are all wet! Can you draw her some new clothes? As you draw the clothes, say their names in French.

Activité Deux

In the appendix are paper dolls and clothes that you can use for this activity. Cut the pieces out, color them, then come back to this page. Use your dolls in this scene. Describe the clothes the dolls are wearing.

Challenge: Speak for each doll telling the other doll what they are wearing. You can use the phrases: *Je porte* (*zhuh-pohrt*) for 'I am wearing' and *Tu porte* (*too-pohrt*) for 'you are wearing'.

Activité Trois

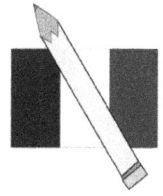

Fill in the missing letters and then draw a line from the picture to the correct French word.

le ch__mi__e

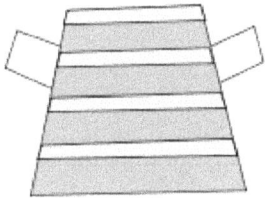

le ju__e

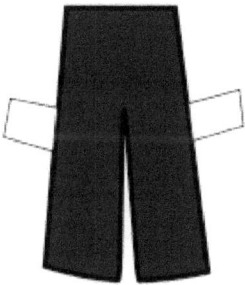

le pan__alon

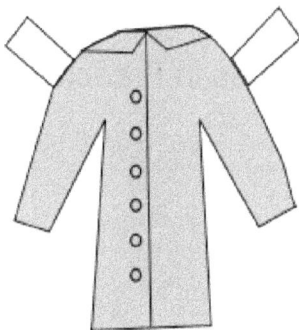

le man__eau

Activité Quatre

Matching Game

You will need:

the matching cards from the back of this workbook
scissors

What to do:

1. Turn the cards upside-down.
2. Turn over two at a time to see if you have a pair of the picture and the correct word in French. If so, put them in a pile; if not, turn them back over and try again.

Challenge:

Every time you make a match of cards, make a complete sentence with the word in French!

Activité Cinq

Pulling it All Together

You will need:

any toys or objects that you have for which you learned their names in this workbook - stuffed baby animals, fairy wings, etc.
backpack

What to do:

1. Put all of the toys and objects in your backpack.
2. Surprise your parents or grandparents. Tell them you have something to show them.
3. Then, one by one, take out each object and say their names in French. Try to make sentences too, if you would like to try.

Appendices

My French Path

Every time you finish a *leçon* in the book, color a section of the learning slide.

1
2
3
4
5
6
7
8
9
10

Three cheers for

Félicitations!
Congratulations!
You have successfully finished
More French for Little Girls.

English to French Dictionary

artist	l'artiste	*lah-teest*
baker	le boulanger	*luh-boo-lahn-zhay*
ballet	le ballet	*leh-bah-lay*
ballet shoes	les chaussures de ballet	*lay-show-soohrs-duh-bah-lay*
beach	la plage	*lah-plahj*
beach ball	la ballon de plage	*lah-ba-lohn-duh-plahj*
bless you	à tes souhaits	*a-tay-soo-ayt*
bracelet	le bracelet	*luh-bras-leht*
breakfast	le petit déjeuner	*luh-peh-tee-day-zhuh-nay*
calf	le veau	*luh-voh*
chick	le poussin	*luh-poo-seh$_n$*
coat	le manteau	*luh-manh-toh*
cook	le cuisinier	*luh-kwee-zee-nyehr*

cycling	le vélo	*luh-vay-loh*
dance	la danse	*lah-dahns*
dessert	le dessert	*luh-deh-sehr*
dinner	le dîner	*luh-dee-nay*
dress	la robe	*lah-rohb*
earring	la boucle d'oreille	*lah-boo-kluh-doh-ray*
ears	les oreilles	*lay-zoh-ray*
eighteen	dix-huit	*deez-weet*
eleven	onze	*ohnz*
excuse me	excusez-moi	*ehks-kyoo-zay-mwah*
eyes	les yeux	*lay-zyuh*
face	le visage	*luh-vee-zahj*
fairy	la fée	*lah-fay*
fifteen	quinze	*kanz*

foal	le poulain	*luh-poo-lahn*
fourteen	quatorze	*ka-tohrz*
gymnastics	la gymnastique	*lah-zhim-nahs-teek*
hair	les cheveux	*lay-shuh-vuh*
hat	le chapeau	*luh-shah-poh*
have a good meal	bon appétit	*bohn-ap-pay-tee*
I'm angry	je suis en colère	*zhuh-sweez-ahn-koh-lehr*
I'm crazy	je suis fou	*zhuh-swee-foo*
I'm happy	je suis contente	*zhuh-swee-kohn-tahnt*
I'm sad	je suis triste	*zhuh-swee-treest*
I cook	je cuisine	*zhuh-kwee-zeen*
I dance	je danse	*zhuh-dahns*
I play	je joue	*zhuh-zhoo*

I swim	je nage	*zhuh-nahj*
I want	je veux	*zhuh-vuh*
ice skating	le patinage sur glace	*luh-pa-tee-nahj-suhr-glass*
jazz dance	la danse jazz	*lah-dahns-jazz*
jewelry	les bijoux	*lay-bee-zhoo*
kitchen	la cuisine	*lah-kwee-zeen*
kitten	le chaton	*luh-sha-tohn*
leotard	le justaucorps	*luh-just-oh-kohr*
lunch	le déjeuner	*luh-day-zhuh-nay*
magic dust	la poussière magique	*lah-poo-syehr-mah-jeek*
maybe	peut-être	*puht-ehtr*
mouth	la bouche	*lah-boosh*
necklace	le collier	*luh-koh-lee-ay*

no	non	*noh*
nose	le nez	*luh-nay*
nice to meet you	enchanté	*ahn-shahn-tay*
nineteen	dix-neuf	*deez-neuhf*
paint	la peinture	*lah-payn-tuhr*
paint brush	le pinceau	*luh-pahn-soh*
painter	la peintre	*lah-payntr*
pants	le pantalon	*luh-pahn-tah-lohn*
pencil	le crayon	*luh-kray-yohn*
puppy	le chiot	*luh-shee-oh*
ring	l'anneau	*lah-noh*
sand	le sable	*luh-sah-bl*
sandcastle	le château de sa-ble	*luh-shah-toh-duh-sah-bl*
sculptor	le sculpteur	*luh-scoolp-tuhr*

sea	la mer	*lah-mehr*
seventeen	dix-sept	*dees-seht*
shell	la coquille	*lah-koh-keel*
shirt	le chemise	*luh-sheh-meez*
sixteen	seize	*sehz*
skirt	la jupe	*lah-zhoop*
soccer	le football	*luh-foot-ball*
sunglasses	les lunettes de soleil	*lay-loo-neht-duh-soh-lay*
swimming	la natation	*lah-nah-tah-seeohn*
tap dance	la danse du robinet	*lah-dahns-doo-roh-bee-nay*
tennis	le tennis	*luh-teh-nees*
thirteen	treize	*thehz*
to dance	danser	*dahn-say*
to make/to do	faire	*fair*

twelve	douze	*dooz*
twenty	vingt	*vah_nt*
very	très	*trey*
wand	le baguette	*luh-bah-geht*
wing	l'aile	*lehl*
yes	oui	*wee*
you cook	tu cuisines	*too-kwee-zeen*
you dance	tu danses	*too-dahns*
you play	tu joues	*too-zhoo*
you swim	tu nages	*too-nahj*
you want	tu veux	*too-vuh*

French to English Dictionary

à tes souhaits	*a-tay-soo-ayt*	bless you
l'aile	*lehl*	wing
l'anneau	*lah-noh*	ring
l'artiste	*lah-teest*	artist
le baguette	*luh-bah-geht*	wand
le ballet	*leh-bah-lay*	ballet
la ballon de plage	*lah-ba-lohn-duh-plahj*	beach ball
les bijoux	*lay-bee-zhoo*	jewelry
la bouche	*lah-boosh*	mouth
la boucle d'oreille	*lah-boo-kluh-doh-ray*	earring
le boulanger	*luh-boo-lahn-zhay*	baker
bon appétit	*bohn-ap-pay-tee*	have a good meal
le bracelet	*luh-bras-leht*	bracelet

le chapeau	*luh-shah-poh*	hat
le château de sa-ble	*luh-sha-toh-duh-sah-bl*	sandcastle
le chaton	*luh-sha-tohn*	kitten
les chaussures de ballet	*lay-show-soohrs-duh-bah-lay*	ballet shoes
le chemise	*luh-sheh-meez*	shirt
les cheveux	*lay-shuh-vuh*	hair
le chiot	*luh-shee-oh*	puppy
le collier	*luh-koh-lee-ay*	necklace
la coquille	*lah-koh-keel*	shell
le crayon	*luh-kray-yohn*	pencil
la cuisine	*lah-kwee-zeen*	kitchen
le cuisinier	*luh-kwee-zee-nyehr*	cook
la danse	*lah-dahns*	dance
danser	*dahn-say*	to dance

la danse du robi-net	*lah-dahns-doo-roh-bee-nay*	tap dance
la danse jazz	*lah-dahns-jazz*	jazz dance
le déjeuner	*luh-day-zhuh-nay*	lunch
le dessert	*luh-deh-sehr*	dessert
le dîner	*luh-dee-nay*	dinner
dix-huit	*deez-weet*	eighteen
dix-neuf	*deez-neuhf*	nineteen
douze	*dooz*	twelve
enchanté	*ahn-shahn-tay*	nice to meet you
excusez-moi	*ehks-kyoo-zay-mwah*	excuse me
faire	*fair*	to make/to do
la fée	*lah-fay*	fairy
le football	*luh-foot-ball*	soccer
la gymnastique	*lah-zhim-nahs-teek*	gymnastics

je cuisine	*zhuh-kwee-zeen*	I cook
je danse	*zhuh-dahns*	I dance
je joue	*zhuh-zhoo*	I play
je nage	*zhuh-nahj*	I swim
je suis contente	*zhuh-swee-kohn-tahnt*	I'm happy
je suis en colère	*zhuh-sweez-ahn-koh-lehr*	I'm angry
je suis fou	*zhuh-swee-foo*	I'm crazy
je suis triste	*zhuh-swee-treest*	I'm sad
je veux	*zhuh-vuh*	I want
la jupe	*lah-zhoop*	skirt
le justaucorps	*luh-just-oh-kohr*	leotard
les lunettes de soleil	*lay-loo-neht-duh-soh-lay*	sunglasses
le manteau	*luh-mahn-toh*	coat
la mer	*lah-mehr*	sea

la natation	*lah-nah-tah-seeohn*	swimming
le nez	*luh-nay*	nose
non	*noh*	no
onze	*ohnz*	eleven
les oreilles	*lay-zoh-ray*	ears
oui	*wee*	yes
le pantalon	*luh-pahn-tah-lohn*	pants
le patinage sur glace	*luh-pa-tee-nahj-suhr-glass*	ice skating
la peintre	*lah-payntr*	painter
la peinture	*lah-payn-tuhr*	paint
le petit déjeuner	*luh-peh-tee-day-zhuh-nay*	breakfast
peut-être	*puht-ehtr*	maybe
le pinceau	*luh-pahn-soh*	paint brush
la plage	*lah-plahj*	beach

le poulain	*luh-poo-lahn*	foal
la poussière magique	*lah-poo-syehr-mah-jeek*	magic dust
le poussin	*luh-poo-sehn*	chick
quatorze	*ka-tohrz*	fourteen
quinze	*kanz*	fifteen
la robe	*lah-rohb*	dress
le sable	*luh-sah-bl*	sand
le sculpteur	*luh-scoolp-tuhr*	sculptor
seize	*sehz*	sixteen
le tennis	*luh-teh-nees*	tennis
treize	*thehz*	thirteen
très	*trey*	very
tu cuisines	*too-kwee-zeen*	you cook
tu danses	*too-dahns*	you dance

tu joues	*too-zhoo*	you play
tu nages	*too-nahj*	you swim
tu veux	*too-vuh*	you want
le veau	*luh-voh*	calf
le vélo	*luh-vay-loh*	cycling
vingt	*vahnt*	twenty
le visage	*luh-vee-zahj*	face
les yeux	*lay-zyuh*	eyes

Bingo

What you will need:

- Bingo cards – in this booklet.
- A hat or a cap.
- Something to cover up the squares on the cards, like dry beans or pennies.

What to do:

1. Cut out the cards on page 87, fold them and put them into a hat.
2. Draw one strip of paper out and say the word with the letter.
3. The children will cover up the word that they heard.
4. Repeat step 4 and 5 until there is a winner!

B	I	N	G	O
		free square		

B	I	N	G	O
		free square		

B	I	N	G	O
		free square		

Cards for Bingo

B - la fée	B - la poussière magique	B - les bijoux	B - la peinture	B - le bracelet
B - la baguette	B - la boucle d'oreille	B - l'aile	B - le collier	B - l'anneau
I - la fée	I - la poussière magique	I - les bijoux	I - la peinture	I - le bracelet
I - la baguette	I - la boucle d'oreille	I - l'aile	I - le collier	I - l'anneau
N - la fée	N - la poussière magique	N - les bijoux	N - la peinture	N - le bracelet
N - la baguette	N - la boucle d'oreille	N - l'aile	N - le collier	N - l'anneau
G - la fée	G - la poussière magique	G - les bijoux	G - la peinture	G - le bracelet
G - la baguette	G - la boucle d'oreille	G - l'aile	G - le collier	G - l'anneau
O - la fée	O - la poussière magique	O - les bijoux	O - la peinture	O - le bracelet
O - la baguette	O - la boucle d'oreille	O - l'aile	O - le collier	O - l'anneau

Matching Game

What to do:

1. Cut out the following cards. Paste them onto cardboard for stability if you would like.
2. Turn the cards upside-down.
3. Turn over two at a time to see if you have a pair of the picture and the correct word in French.

le baguette

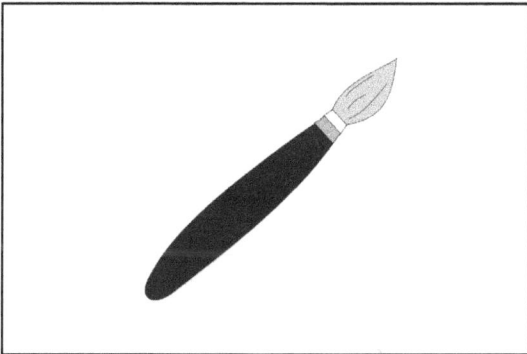

le pinceau

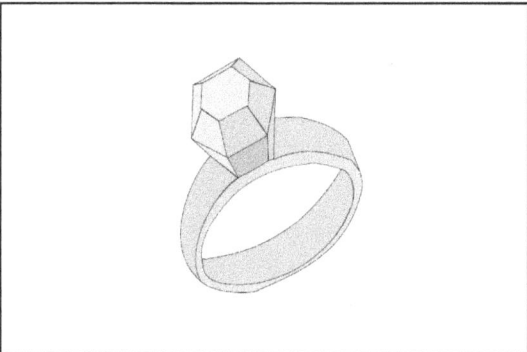

l'anneau

	la fée
	le poulain
	la gymnastique
	la danse jazz

	les yeux
	le cuisinier
	le pantalon
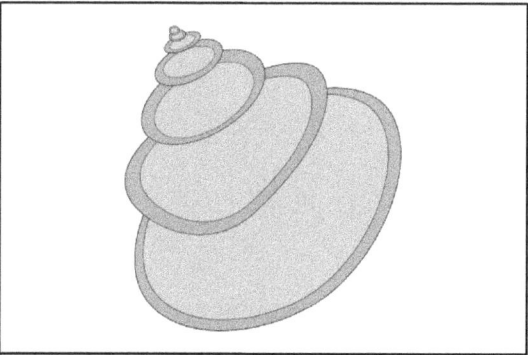	la coquille

Paper Dolls